watch it grow

by Ivan Bulloch & Diane James

Photography Daniel Pangbourne

Illustrations Emily Hare

TWO CAN™

LONDON ■ PRINCETON

www.two-canpublishing.com

Published by Two-Can Publishing,
43-45 Dorset Street, London W1U 7NA

© Two-Can Publishing 2001, 1998

For information on Two-Can books and multimedia,
call (0)20 7224 2440, fax (0)20 7224 7005,
or visit our website at http://www.two-canpublishing.com

Created by

act-two

346 Old Street
London EC1V 9RB

Art Director Ivan Bulloch
Editor Diane James
Design Assistant David Oh
Editorial Assistant Katherine Harvey
Gardening Consultant Sue Hook

With thanks to Jimmy and Winsome James for letting us use their garden
and also Jackie Hyde, Sue Gibbs, Nicky, Katie, George and Sam

'Two-Can' is a trademark of Two-Can Publishing.
Two-Can Publishing is a division of Zenith Entertainment Ltd
43-45 Dorset Street, London W1U 7NA

ISBN 1-85434-921-X

Dewey Decimal Classification 635

Hardback 4 6 8 10 9 7 5 3

A catalogue record for this book is available from the British Library

Printed in Hong Kong

contents

watch it grow

Gardening can be hard work, but it's great fun, too. The exciting thing about being a gardener is that there is always something happening.

Gardeners love talking about their plants! You can learn a lot by listening; chatting to friends who enjoy gardening; looking at gardening books; exploring other gardens and visiting garden centres. The scarecrow in this book has plenty of good advice, too!

Work, watch and enjoy.

Once you start growing your own plants you won't want to stop gardening, even if you haven't got much space.
Have fun!

big & small

Plants are living things, just like people. They come in lots of different shapes and sizes – from the tallest tree to the tiniest flower. Some plants can survive cold, windy conditions, others need warmth and shelter. All plants need light, food, air and water. They like to be looked after, too! Before you begin gardening, here are some things you need to know.

flower
leaf
stem
root

Growing up Nearly all plants grow from either seeds or bulbs. Each seed contains enough food for a plant to start growing, but the seed also needs soil and water. When you plant a seed in soil, it grows roots which push downwards. The roots anchor the plant in the soil and take in water and food from it. The seed pushes a stem and leaves above the soil. The leaves use sunlight and carbon dioxide, a gas in the air, to make food to help the plant grow.

Read and discover You can buy seeds in packets or you can buy ready-grown plants. Read the instructions on the packets or labels to find out how big the plants will grow, when to plant them and how long they will live.

These bulbs will make a colourful display when it is too cold for other plants to grow.

Planning There is a huge range of plants to choose from. Think about colours, shapes and which ones will look good together.
You should also bear in mind how much space you have got!

Annuals These are plants that 'visit' the garden. They are easy to grow from seeds, but flower and die in the same year. You'll find lots of annuals in garden centres as ready-to-grow plants.

Brightly coloured annuals look good in pots and window boxes.

Trees are the tallest plants. They provide shade and shelter for all kinds of animals. This apple tree will also provide delicious fruit that you can eat.

Biennials These grow from seeds into young plants one year, then flower and die the following year.

Perennials These flowering plants grow from seeds and come up year after year. They disappear in winter but shoot up again when the weather warms up in spring.

Bulbs A bulb has layers of fleshy leaves which contain food for the growing plant. Some bulbs push strong, green shoots above the soil, even in cold, frosty weather.

Shrubs You can recognise a shrub by its woody stem and chunky shape. The plant on the right is a small shrub.

Trees These giants of the plant world live longer than anything else in the garden. They need a lot of space for their long, strong roots and branches to spread out.

7

tips & tools

When you start gardening, you'll only need a few basic tools. You can get more equipment as your garden grows bigger! Good tools will last for years if you take care of them. Be very careful of sharp edges!

Trowel Use this for digging in small spaces, such as pots and window boxes. A trowel can also be used to dig out the roots of stubborn weeds in the garden.

Rake Use this to level the soil, comb off stones and break up the surface into fine crumbs. A rake with long, thin prongs is good for scraping leaves from the lawn.

Watering can This is important, especially during dry weather. Plants need a good soaking, not a sprinkle, to stop them drooping! Watering cans have a fine 'rose' over the spout so that the water showers out gently. In a large garden, use a hose to water in early morning or early evening. Collect rainwater in a water butt.

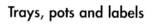

Trays, pots and labels
Use seed trays to grow plants from seeds. Small pots are useful for seedlings or cuttings before they are planted in the garden. Use labels if you think you might forget what you have planted!

Fork A small fork will help with the same jobs as a trowel, especially weeding. Use it to break up the soil, too.

Sticks Use long bamboo sticks to keep tall plants upright. Poke one into the soil next to the plant and tie the stem of the plant to it.

Tie it up Support plants by tying them to sticks with soft string, or garden twine.

Never eat anything from the garden without asking a grown-up first! Many plants are poisonous.

Spade A spade with a long handle is best for turning soil over to break up lumps. It is also useful for digging large holes to plant trees and shrubs. Clean your spade and all your garden tools before you put them away.

Berries are for animals only!

More haste, less speed Don't rush jobs in the garden. Take your time or you may damage plants and even yourself. Try to finish one job before you start the next.

Clothes Gardening clothes should be comfortable and practical. Gardening gloves will help to stop blisters and cuts. Always wash your hands after gardening.

9

seed sowing

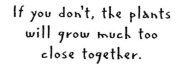

Growing your own plants from seeds is extremely satisfying! Look at the pictures on seed packets and choose your favourites. The instructions will tell you when, where and how deep to sow the seeds, indoors or outdoors, how long they will take to grow, and how tall and wide they will be when they are fully grown plants.

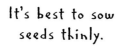

It's best to sow seeds thinly.

If you don't, the plants will grow much too close together.

Seed trays Buy plastic seed trays, or make holes in the bottom of empty food containers and egg boxes. You can put your trays on a windowsill indoors, or in a greenhouse in the garden. Some trays are sold with protective covers.

Patience! It may be several weeks before you see the seedlings appear, although some seeds grow very quickly. Check them daily. Make sure that the soil is moist and the trays are not in direct sunlight. Some seeds need to grow in darkness. If you have put a protective cover over the seeds, take it off when you see the first green seedlings.

Indoors or outdoors? Some seeds can be sown outdoors. Make sure you prepare their space first. Dig and rake the soil to get rid of lumps and stones and to make a level surface.

how to do it

1 Fill a seed tray, nearly to the top, with compost and level the surface. Water the compost using a watering can with a fine rose.

2 Sprinkle the seeds on the surface. Cover them with a thin layer of compost. Use a spray to moisten the compost without disturbing the seeds.

Growing bigger! Keep a careful eye on your new seedlings. Don't let the compost dry out. Turn to the next page to find out what to do next.

Soil for seeds Use a seed compost which you can buy at garden centres. This has all the food your seeds need to start them off. It is similar to buying special food for babies!

3 Cover the seed tray with a clear plastic cover, or clingfilm, to protect the seeds. Put the tray in a warm, light place. Label the tray.

moving on

When your seeds have pushed their way up through the soil and grown leaves, they are called seedlings.

Now they need more space to grow. Moving seedlings to a new home is called pricking out. Treat them carefully and your seedlings will grow into strong, healthy plants. Give any spare seedlings to your friends.

1 Fill a seed tray, or pots, with compost. Water the tray and level the surface. Use a plastic plant label, or a tool called a widger, to help separate out a small clump of seedlings from the rest. Hold the leaves of one seedling and gently pull it away from the others.

Time to move Check your trays every day. The first two leaves that a seedling grows are called seed leaves. Don't be surprised, the next leaves will look quite different! When the seedlings look crowded or straggly, it's time to prick them out.

2 Make a small hole in the compost with the plant label, or widger. Put the seedling in and firm the soil around it. Give each seedling's roots plenty of room. Now water the trays and pots using a fine rose or spray.

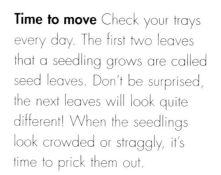

Weather watch! In late spring when the weather is warm and there is no frost, you can put your pricked-out seedlings outside for a few hours during the day. This is called hardening off and it prepares the seedlings for being planted in the garden.

Planting out Treat seedlings bought from a garden centre in the same way as seedlings you have grown. Prepare the soil by breaking up lumps with a fork. Pull up any weeds, then rake the surface to even it out. Make a hole large enough for each new plant. Support the plant with both hands, then put it into the hole. Push soil gently around the plant. Follow up with a good watering.

Give each new plant plenty of space to grow upwards and spread outwards.

Don't plant your seedlings out too soon.
Wait until they have strong roots.

Check the packet to find out how tall your plants will grow.

Put tall plants towards the back of the flowerbed.

13

planting bulbs

One of the best known bulbs is the onion we eat! Lots of flowering plants also grow from bulbs. Favourites are the brave, colourful bulbs that push their way through frosty ground to let us know that warmer weather is on its way! You can grow bulbs in flowerbeds or containers. Some bulbs are happy to grow indoors.

Top and bottom Sometimes it is tricky to tell which way up to plant a bulb. Usually, the pointed end produces the growing shoot and the flat end produces the roots. With small bulbs you may not be able to tell the difference. If in doubt, plant the bulb on its side. As a general rule, plant bulbs twice as deep as their height.

Look for bulbs that are heavy, fattish and not badly marked or mouldy.

When to plant? The best time to plant most bulbs is late summer. Many bulbs don't like being out of soil for long periods, so try to buy them when you have time to plant them straightaway.

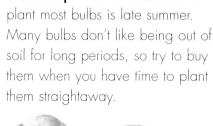

It is easy to see the roots on this bulb!

Leave your bulbs in the ground and they will spread and come up year after year.

Bulb planter This is a special tool to help you plant bulbs, especially if you want them to push up through your lawn. Use it to remove a small, circular plug of soil and turf. Plant the bulb in the hole and replace the turf.

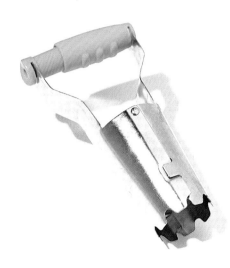

Next year's food When a bulb has finished flowering, don't cut back straggly leaves. Be patient and wait until they go brown. The bulb's leaves make food for the next year's growth.

Where did I put it? Label your bulbs as soon as you have planted them. This will help to stop you digging them up before the leaves and flowers appear above the soil.

how to do it

1 Plant a container with bulbs to make a colourful spring display on an outdoor windowsill or patio. Put small pebbles in the bottom to help water drain away.

2 Half fill the container with compost. Place the bulbs, roots down, on top of the compost. Put them close together, but not touching.

3 Cover the bulbs with more compost. Some can have their tips showing. Make sure the compost is moist, but not soggy, or the bulbs will rot.

under control

When you have planted your seeds, bulbs and new plants, don't think you can sit back and have a rest. There are lots more jobs to do in the garden! Try to keep things neat and tidy every day so that the work doesn't pile up.

Save water! Collect rainwater in buckets and use it to give your thirsty plants a drink.

Thirsty work On hot, sunny days, the soil soon dries out and plants need a drink. Nothing is as good as a shower of rain, but you can help. Wait until early evening and give everything a good soaking. Direct the water at the bottom of plants so that you don't waste it and damage flower heads. Remember the plants in pots, too!

Look out! When you are doing different jobs in the garden, keep an eye out for damage caused by garden pests. Look for tell-tale holes in leaves, discoloured leaves and droopy plants. Can you see what is causing the damage? You'll find some tips to help you deal with trouble-makers on pages 22 and 23.

Use a hose for large flowerbeds and lawns, and a watering can for small areas.

Tie up plants carefully. Very tall plants will need securing in several places.

Stand up! Tall plants with heavy blooms will droop over if you don't give them support. Before they grow tall, poke a stick into the soil beside each plant. Tie the stem to the stick.

Spick and span General jobs include raking up dead leaves and keeping borders neat and tidy. Dead-heading is also important. This means cutting off flower heads when they have finished flowering. It encourages more flowers to grow.

Weed it out A weed is any plant growing where you don't want it. Some plants have long, spreading roots which take food away from other plants. Some even wrap themselves around other plants, eventually strangling them. Make sure you get rid of all the roots of an unwanted weed. If you don't, before you know it, the weed will grow back again.

If you've got a big garden, share the jobs with friends who like gardening!

All year round There always seem to be more jobs in the summer when the garden is in full bloom. Tidying and keeping an eye on things are important, even in winter when there is not much growing.

Dig around weeds and pull them up gently with their roots. You may have to dig deep.

tastes good!

how to do it

There is nothing more delicious than eating home-grown vegetables and fruit. You don't need a lot of space to grow plants to eat. Many will be quite happy in containers. When the weather is sunny and there is no danger of frost, try growing some tasty runner beans in a big pot.

1 Make a runner-bean wigwam in a large pot, or in the garden. Push three sticks into the soil and tie them at the top to make a pyramid. Plant a bean seed, or bean plant, at the bottom of each stick.

2 As the plants climb, wind them round each stick. After a couple of months you will see red flowers which will turn into beans. When the beans are about 10 cm long and snap easily, they are ready.

Tomatoes need a lot of water, especially on sunny days. When the fruits appear, give them a special feed (see page 25).

Ready to eat? The parts of vegetables that you eat grow below the soil and above. Test vegetables growing underground by digging one up. Tiny carrots taste sweet and delicious. Don't let them grow big and woody.

Protect young vegetable plants or the birds will eat them!

The fruits can become heavy. Support your tomato plant by tying it in different places to one or more sticks.

A whole meal! Plants for salads are delicious and easy to grow in spring. Buy tomato, lettuce and radish seeds. Read the instructions on the packet and sow your seeds in the garden, or in pots. Or try a grow-bag – a huge plastic bag filled with compost. Cut a hole in the top and pop in your plants.

Dig up root vegetables carefully so that you don't damage them. If you are left with too many vegetables, don't forget your friends and neighbours.

Pick the fruits as soon as they are ripe. Wash them and eat them straightaway to get the best taste!

Always fresh Vegetables and fruits grow at different times of the year. Some, such as lettuces and tomatoes, prefer sunny weather, others, like potatoes, can brave winter frosts. Work out a timetable using the information on seed packets and you will have something fresh every day.

herbs

Herbs are another kind of plant you can eat. They add amazing flavour to your cooking and to salads. Herbs often taste and smell quite strong, so you only need to use a few leaves at a time. For hundreds of years, people have used herbs as a cure for different illnesses – from colds and headaches, to bruises and tummy aches. They are good-looking plants, too. Always ask a grown-up to tell you if a herb is safe to eat.

Happy together Many herbs grow well in dry, stony soil. Choose a sunny patch of ground, or a large pot, and plant a selection of herbs. Traditional herb gardens are often planted so that the herbs grow in patterns. Herbs can be planted in an area on their own, or in flowerbeds with other plants.

Pinch off the tops of the growing shoots.

Stop your herbs growing tall and straggly.

All year round To make sure you have fresh herbs in winter, sow seeds in small pots towards the end of summer. Keep them on the kitchen windowsill and snip leaves off when you need them. For an even bigger supply, harvest herbs from the garden and dry them.

how to do it

1 Try drying herbs so you have a supply when they are not growing. Pick bunches of your favourite herbs. Tie them with garden twine or raffia. Remove leaves that are damaged or discoloured.

2 Hang the bunches in a dry, airy room – or airing cupboard – and leave them for a couple of weeks. When the herbs are completely dry they will feel slightly crackly.

Tastes good! Try experimenting by adding herbs to food to find out which flavours you like best. Chopping or tearing fresh herbs into small pieces releases the flavour and makes it easy to scatter them evenly.

3 Take the dry leaves off the stems and rub them into tiny pieces. Put them in clean, dry jars with screwtops. Label each jar. Dry herbs taste stronger than fresh ones, so you don't need to use as much of them.

know your friends

Gardens are full of other living things, as well as plants! It's good to know which creatures to encourage to share your garden, and which ones may damage your plants. A bit of detective work will sort out the good guys from the baddies!

Slugs and snails These slippery creatures love to feed on plants and can do a lot of damage. The best way to stop them is to put up barriers. You can protect young plants by surrounding them with a collar cut from a plastic bottle. Or, cover the surface of the soil around the plant with broken eggshells. Keep a special eye on young seedlings.

Grow plants that provide food for insects such as butterflies.

Worms are a gardener's best friend. They work day and night to turn over the soil.

Making seeds Flowers must be pollinated before they can make new seeds, which in turn grow into new plants. Insects carry a special powder found in plants, called pollen, from one flower to another. The patterns on flower petals guide the insects to the pollen which is in the middle of the flower. Pollen carriers are important. Look out for bees with thick powder on their legs!

Friends Ladybirds, hedgehogs, frogs and toads all feed on harmful insects and will not damage your plants.

Slugs and snails hate crawling over anything prickly or sharp – like eggshells!

how to do it

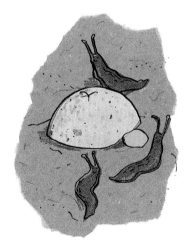

1 Pests love to hide in dark places. Keep your garden clean and tidy. Don't leave piles of leaves, bits of wood or stacks of old flowerpots where pests can hide and multiply.

Don't forget that birds need water as well as food. They need your help most in the cold winter months when they cannot find their favourite meal of worms and insects.

Feathered friends No garden is complete without the sound of birds, but you may have to put up with a bit of damage! Birds like to nibble young shoots and buds. In return, they are happy to gobble up slugs, snails, caterpillars and bugs that may damage your plants.

Spraying Think twice before using a chemical spray to get rid of pests. You may harm some of the creatures that your garden needs. Spray the culprits with soapy water, or pick them off the plants by hand. If you spot the problem soon enough, you can act before the bugs eat your plants.

2 Prop up an empty grapefruit with a small stone. Slugs will shelter under it. Pick up the grapefruit with the slugs inside and put it out of harm's way!

3 Look for caterpillars on leaves. Lift them off gently with your fingers and put them where they can't do any damage!

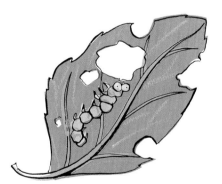

Give plants a soapy soaking, paying attention to the undersides of the leaves.

planting in pots

You don't need to have a garden to enjoy growing plants! Pots and tubs come in many different shapes and sizes and will fit into all sorts of spaces.

What to plant Most plants – from a tiny herb to a bushy shrub – will grow in a container. Find out how tall and wide each plant will grow and choose a big enough pot. Try growing different kinds of plants in the same pot.

What sort of pot The ideal pot is waterproof and will stand firmly on the ground without wobbling. It should have at least one hole in the bottom to allow water to drain through. Most plants do not like to grow in waterlogged soil.

Looking after pots Plants growing in pots need the same amount of care as plants growing in the garden. Make sure the soil does not dry out and check for pests! Look out for nipped off buds and holes in leaves.

Use a large tin to make an instant container. Ask a grown-up to punch drainage holes in the bottom. Don't try to do it yourself!

Plants in pots need watering more often than those in the garden!

Grouping Think about the best way to display your flower pots. Try having one large central pot and surrounding it with smaller ones. What about several single flower pots in a row, perhaps on a window ledge?

Feed me Because pot plants grow in less soil than those in the garden, they sometimes need an extra feed to help them grow. You can buy special plant food in garden centres which you need to add when you are watering. Make sure you read the instructions on the packet carefully.

how to do it

1 Put some crocks (broken flower pots), or a layer of gravel, in the bottom of the container to improve drainage. Pour in compost to about half-way for large plants and higher for small ones. Place the pot on an old saucer or plant tray.

2 Gently separate the roots of the plants and place them in position. Use a trowel to fill in compost round the plants. Leave a small space at the top of the container. If you don't, the water will spill over. Now water your plants well.

Bold and bright arrangements look colourful and jolly, pale and dark shades of one colour look calm and peaceful.

Two planks of wood and a few bricks make a platform to display pots at different heights and also save on space.

free plants!

You don't have to spend any money to grow plants! Lots can be grown from cuttings. With care, and luck, you can take a piece of an adult plant and grow a new one from it. Shrubs and trees grow much quicker from cuttings than from seed. You can also collect and grow seeds from plants that have finished flowering, or from fruit you have eaten.

Hit and miss Don't be upset if some of of your cuttings don't grow. Take about twice as many cuttings as you need and you will end up with plenty of plants – and probably some to spare!

Swap seeds and cuttings with your friends.

Hard and soft Soft cuttings are taken in early summer from young, fleshy shoots. Hard cuttings are taken in autumn from older, woody stems. An easy method is known as a heel cutting. Choose a healthy-looking side shoot – hard or soft without flowers – and pull it downwards, away from the main stem. The extra bit left at the bottom looks a bit like a heel.

Full speed ahead You can take cuttings in early summer or in autumn. Gather your cuttings as quickly as possible and pop them in a plastic bag to protect them. Plant your cuttings straightaway.

Take heel cuttings from healthy side shoots. Plant them in compost as soon as possible.

how to do it

1 Almost fill small flowerpots with compost. Water them well. Use the end of a pencil to make a small hole for each cutting. Strip the bottom leaves off the cutting and poke it into the hole. Firm the soil around the stem.

2 You can put more than one cutting in each pot but make sure they have plenty of space. Tie a polythene bag over the pot, or use an up-turned jam jar, taking care not to touch the cuttings. This will help to keep the soil moist.

3 Put the pot out of direct sunlight. Keep the compost damp, not soggy. After two or three weeks take the bag off and keep an eye on your new plants. Outdoor cuttings can be planted in the garden when they have strong roots.

Have a go! Some cuttings will grow from a single leaf and its stem. Choose a plant with a large, healthy leaf like the one below. Cut off a single leaf with a bit of stem. Poke the stem into a pot of compost. If you are lucky, after about a month, you will see a new plant growing from the bottom of the leaf.

A quick drink Another way to try your luck is to pop a cutting into a glass of water. Keep the glass in a light place and watch to see if roots grow from the bottom of the stem. If they do, plant the cutting in a pot of compost as you did before.

Seed bank Another way to save money is to collect seeds from dry flower seed heads in late summer. Keep them in a labelled paper bag and sow them in spring.

a perfect bunch

Picking flowers and leafy stems from the garden and making them into a colourful arrangement can really cheer up a room – they often smell lovely, too! A bunch of cut flowers makes a good present, especially if you have grown them yourself.

Try to keep flowers away from hot sun when you have picked them.

Don't pick wild flowers in the countryside.

They are for everyone to enjoy.

What colour? It's best to have a plan before you start picking flowers. Have a look round to see what is available and decide which colours you like best.

Don't pick all the flowers in the garden, leave some so that you can enjoy them indoors *and* outdoors!

Pick the best Look for flowers that are about to bloom. They will last longer when you take them indoors. Use a pair of scissors to cut the flower stems close to the bottom. Try to put the cut flowers into water as soon as possible.

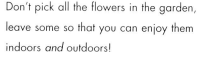

The right vase You can use any container for a flower arrangement, as long as it is waterproof. A simple jam jar, a small bucket or even an old teapot all work well.

Keep still! Here are a few tricks to keep your arrangement in place. You can buy a special type of foam from flower shops. Cut it to fit the bottom of your vase and fill the vase with water. Push the flower stems into the wet foam. Another method to keep the stems in place is to fill the bottom of the vase with marbles before poking in the flower stems.

Find a container in a colour that will look good with your flower colours and you can't go wrong!

how to do it

1 Choose a tall vase for long stems or a small one for short stems. Put a piece of foam, or some marbles in the bottom. Almost fill the vase with water.

2 Start with the longest stems and push them into the middle. Then fill in around the edges with the shorter stems.

Longer lasting To keep your arrangement fresh for as long as possible, strip the bottom leaves off the stems before you put them in water. If you don't they will rot and the flowers will die. Take out single stems as they die off. Change the water every few days.

indoor plants

Growing plants indoors is just as satisfying as growing them in the garden. You can have a colourful display in the middle of winter when there is little growing outside. Garden centres and supermarkets sell indoor plants. Read the instructions on the pot to find out how to take care of your new plant.

When you go on holiday, give your indoor plants to a friend for safekeeping.

All sizes You can buy plants to suit any space – small plants for narrow windowsills or huge ones to fill up a dull corner. Try grouping plants together to make a colourful display.

Not too much! Indoor plants need watering just like those outside, but not too much. Water them about once a week in summer and less in winter when they are not growing. Put your pots on a saucer, or in a bowl slightly larger than the pot. Don't leave plants sitting in water.

The best place Indoor plants like light, but not direct sunlight which will burn their leaves and dry out the soil. Don't put your plants in a drafty position.

how to do it

1 Don't let your plants become dusty! Gently brush leaves with a soft brush. You can buy leaf shine wipes which are useful for cleaning big, waxy leaves.

2 Use a water spray to perk up your plants during hot weather. Spray a fine mist on to the leaves, but don't spray the furniture!

Summer holiday On hot, sunny days, most indoor plants will enjoy a spell outside. Prickly cacti are especially fond of sunny days, probably because they are most at home in the desert! Handle them carefully.

index